From Student to Entrepreneur

Making a Transition to Business

CORY ROBERSON

First Edition
Printed in the United States of America

ISBN: 1512079774
ISBN-13: 9781512079777
Library of Congress Control Number: 2015907595

CONTENTS

Charge for the Young Generation

In the United States and in some other countries, the cost of living is rising, student debt is high, low-paying jobs are common, and unemployment figures are high. Many students, especially those who are between the ages of sixteen and thirty-five years old, are adversely affected. On one hand, these circumstances can be beneficial: students must work harder to become successful. On the other hand, some are forced to live paycheck to paycheck. It's not uncommon to hear of young people working two or even three jobs to make ends meet.

My hope is that you—student, graduate, young person—can find a path toward ownership of a business, land, property, or other assets. Whatever path you choose, success will depend on your ability to create a plan that generates money.

The path to business ownership is an emotional journey. This book will cover some of the challenges that many of us entrepreneurs face—experiences that aren't covered in the standard business curriculum. Every entrepreneur will have different experiences, so use this material as a general guide for your road to success.

Making a transition from student to entrepreneur involves following a stripped-down version of the business-planning process. Inside, you will find ten practical steps (in no particular order) to help you wrap your brain around the world of entrepreneurship.

We Support Youth!

A portion of the proceeds from this book will go toward Build-Ur-Impact, a social enterprise that provides youth and young adults with a path toward ownership through teaching entrepreneurship. Our goal is to offer a standardized curriculum and resource network for budding entrepreneurs.

Disclaimer

Carefully examine what is most appropriate for your own situation. I am not responsible for nor can we be held liable for any decision users make after reading this material. This book is based on what worked for me—it may or may not work for you. Take what you need, and then follow your own path. All the questions that you need answered will not be in this book—this is a general guide only.

Have Questions?

Good entrepreneurs ask many questions. If you don't understand a concept, feel free to send me an e-mail at cory@buildurimpact.com.

Introduction

Starting a business is like making a fishing net to throw out on the lake to catch the next meal.

Entrepreneurs find a path to owning something. There's something to be proud of when working toward this goal. After all, this is a part of the American dream: work hard and get a piece of the pie. For most people, this process starts with a home purchase. For others, including me, this opportunity comes through owning a business. A business, like a home, is an asset that either goes up or down in value (or sometimes stays flat). A business that you own is like your baby: feed it and it will grow. In addition, a successful business can provide you and your family with a source of income and something to sell later on. It's worth it to own something.

What Is Ownership?

Business owners have equity in their companies. What is equity? It's a measure of ownership in an asset, such as a home or business. Business owners may own 100 percent or less, depending on the setup. Their job is to drive up the value of their companies by providing products or services to customers. **Tip**: Those products or services must be things that people want to buy.

Business owners are constantly being tested. The challenge will

3

be sticking to working on the business when life gets tough. This path is not for everyone. Becoming a business owner requires a large amount of sacrifice—think of working two shifts on a job all the time. In the beginning, the business is delicate, unstable, and in need of a significant amount of time—like a newborn baby. Those who are not accustomed to ownership must learn to make this transition to be successful.

More of a Producer Than a Consumer

Entrepreneurs are both producers and consumers. The goal for entrepreneurs is to produce more than they consume. The difference is profit. Whether we like it or not, all of us who are breathing are consumers—it's part of life. From the moment of birth, we use resources that cost money. Upon reaching adulthood, most of us are required to secure income (jobs) to pay for the bare essentials, such as food, water, and clothes. For a business owner, these costs are on top of business expenses. No need to get discouraged; consumerism is a good thing that can work in favor of the business. This means that if your idea has the right products, services, and marketing, someone will want to purchase things from you.

College Grads in Trouble

The economy needs entrepreneurs who can identify and solve problems. When I wrote this book, my task was to identify a problem. I chose to address issues such as the rising cost of college and the lack of adequate employment opportunities for graduates.

According to a 2015 CNN report by David Wheeler titled "Silicon Valley to Millennials: Drop Dead," only 36 percent of college grads have jobs that pay at least $45,000, a sharp decline from the 1990s (after adjusting for inflation). This means that 64 percent of grads have to pay back student loans, pay rent, and make a living on less than $45,000 a year. This is tough in parts of the country like

Silicon Valley, where rent for a one-bedroom apartment can exceed $2,500, approximately two-thirds of these workers' gross monthly income. Many graduates will start out 1) living with their parents, 2) getting roommates, or 3) moving farther away in the hopes of finding a job. Those who can't cope become homeless or live in undesirable places. If not addressed, these problems will continue to threaten this generation's ability to own businesses, homes, and property and to make other forms of progress in our country.

Entrepreneurship and College Debt

According to projectonstudentdebt.org, seven out of ten college seniors (71 percent) who graduated last year had student loan debt, with an average of $29,400 per borrower. Those graduates who are fortunate to get their first jobs will have to pay back loans (and bills) with after-tax dollars. For example, a $45,000 gross salary, subject to taxes of say 20 percent, would leave them with $36,000 net. Paying other bills, such as $15,000 for rent, $2,000 for utilities, $4,000 for a car, $6,000 for food, and $7,000 for other expenses, totals $34,000. That leaves about $2,000 to pay student loan minimums, which will stretch out interest and payments for years. This is the scenario facing many of the 64 percent of grads making less than $45,000 (or $36,000 estimated net after taxes). This can certainly hamper someone who wants to start a business.

Discouraged? Don't be—use this simple analysis as fuel to work on your business ideas. We know that paying back debt requires earning money. At first, you may need to get a job to start paying back that debt. A wise option is to save money and work on that business idea simultaneously. For those who choose another path, you may have to secure other means, such as a loan, or start off with no money. At any rate, stay as lean (cheap) as possible.

A Case for Entrepreneurship

Entrepreneurship is about giving business owners *a bridge from graduation to market opportunities*.

Tip: Build a business that grabs a piece of your target market (customers). Starting a business is like making a fishing net to throw out on the lake to catch the next meal. You don't catch fish—then you don't eat (aside from with the help of charitable support, of course).

The First Job?

A job (or internship) working for someone can be useful. Most of you will soon be starting that first job—unless you were a fifteen-year-old whiz kid entrepreneur, which is possible in this day and age. That first job is a good step, as you'll be gaining some skills and money. If you also have business goals, you can work on them on the side. Think of the first (or second) job as the training ground for your future business endeavors. After all, how do you expect to create your own business unless you've learned how to work somewhere? I did—and wouldn't be in business if I didn't pick up the basic skills required on a job.

Graduated High School or College?

For some, college is a good place to learn how to study and work. For others, it may not be. A college education is a valuable resource for building skills, but it alone may not set up someone with a job. Furthermore, if the next generation doesn't step up and create businesses, there might not be enough jobs to meet the market demand. There aren't statistics behind this claim, but as existing businesses grow and become more efficient, they tend to need fewer people than before. Entrepreneurs work to meet a market demand—and ultimately can grow it.

Finding a Job Is a Job

If you don't start a business, you will search for a career (unless you're taking some sort of break period). When was the last time you talked to a friend or family member who was seeking a job, wanted to leave a job, or just got laid off from a job? For some of you, these conversations happen all the time. The common theme may revolve around pay, working conditions, or treatment from the boss. At the beginning of 2015, I heard from at least four friends and family members who were either laid off or had work-related issues.

Getting another job is not easy. Employers require a number of things: a specified list of skills, no work gaps, and four rounds of interviews, etc. After you go through this application process, there is usually a waiting period of weeks or months before the final decision is made. The background, credit, and every other kind of check must happen before you are hired. But if the job doesn't work out, it takes only one brief fifteen-minute HR meeting to get the pink slip.

The economy also plays a factor in the hiring process. Employers can't hire you if there is no money in their budgets. For example, during the last financial crisis, many school districts around the country laid off teachers because of a lack of funds.

Skills to Pay the Bills

Entrepreneurs need skills and information to get started. Just as they can pose a barrier when you are seeking a job, limited skills can be a barrier to get your foot in the door of any business. As such, don't expect to be paid if you bring no skills to the table.

Entrepreneurs are not entitled to money; they must work hard to find it and earn it. Customers will want a certain quality of products or services delivered before they will spend their money. What should you do about skills? While in school or at a job, you can start to assess what skills you need to get that business up and running.

Tip: Remember the basic skills first.

Before writing a paper on a computer, you must learn how to

type. Before solving a math problem, you must learn how to add. Before starting a business, you must fill out the right paperwork. Before speaking to a client, you must first become versed in the needs of the business. Before developing an app, you must learn how to code in a particular language.

Those with adequate skills could step out into entrepreneurship full time. Others will need to build skills they can use for future jobs.

Shift from Worker to Owner

An entrepreneur must take on the roles of *an employer and a worker.* Even if you don't succeed, you will learn many things that you can bring to any job.

A business requires multiple skills. Other people may have the gift of math, the gift of sciences, or the gift of teaching. You, the entrepreneur, will need to have the gift of vision, looking at the big picture and devising a strategy. You must have the ability to refine your idea and convince someone to buy it.

Entrepreneurs take on multiple roles. They have to be (or outsource) the accounting, sales, technology, and even administrative demands of the business. This can be overwhelming for the one-person team that consists of *you.*

The One-(Wo)Man Shop Complex

Starting off alone? According to an August 2011 Business Insider article titled "18 Amazing Facts about Small Businesses in America," 70 percent of businesses are run by one person. As a small owner, be careful not to diminish your business idea to just a side hustle, hobby, or something to do while you're applying for a "real" job. The idea may be more than that. An entrepreneur may first work as a freelancer, contractor, or consultant. But even freelancers with multiple contracts are operating a business as soon as they start making money. Remember: entrepreneurs don't need a huge staff to be a legitimate business.

Establishing a Brand

Entrepreneurs must think of every angle to build their businesses. Look at the average celebrity who creates a brand. Most start out in one area and then move to another. Every piece of publicity has a purpose. Behind the scenes, entrepreneurs are looking at the next thing to add to their brand (platform).

Puff Daddy is a classic example of a successful entrepreneur who developed a brand. He's known for Bad Boy Records and for launching the career of Notorious Big and many other artists. As his record label was booming, Puffy had the foresight to launch a clothing label—Sean Jean. Since launching his brand, Puffy is now connected to more ventures than most of us will probably ever know about. Some of his business ideas probably failed at some point. But it didn't matter if one venture didn't work; he placed enough bets with multiple businesses. Entrepreneurs like Puff Daddy refuse to be defined by one thing—and so should you.

Entrepreneurship: Is This for You?

Entrepreneurship may not be the path for you. Many entrepreneurs fail at certain points. If you are seeking to be different, you can be that at a job or career. If you are trying to succeed by following a popular trend, you must understand that entrepreneurship can be expensive and time-consuming. If you have a lot of ideas and are willing to put in the work to test them, then this path could be for you. Are you ready to believe in it?

Resources/Materials

Build-Ur-Impact has resources available to support and motivate you to start a business:

Website: www.buildurimpact.com
Blog: http://blog.buildurimpact.com
Questions? info@buildurimpact.com
Resources: www.buildurimpact.com/resources

Workbook Questions:

Answer the questions at the end of each chapter to help you to apply this material to your own situation.

#1

Believe in Yourself

Passion is the emotion and the action is the result.

Entrepreneurs must demonstrate passion. The level of determination to succeed must be greater than the obstacles (time, debt, fear, money, etc.).

Many entrepreneurs face tough periods—this is a safe claim to make. At some point, they find themselves questioning aspects of their business. This is normal because their vision is not yet realized, and some concerns (or a lack of profit) may be present. Most people, including myself, become discouraged by the amount of work required to build a profitable business. Obstacles are common and should be expected.

Those who face opposition or other barriers may quit when they get to the point of having doubts like the following: "I can't do this!" "This is too much work." "I can't afford this." "I can't make money like this." When this happens to you, keep moving forward and discover the root of your problem. Are you quitting because there are legitimate obstacles to your business? Are you quitting because you don't have the work ethic to continue when the going gets rough?

Entrepreneurs cannot control everything in their businesses or the response of the market. Ultimately, business owners will find out whether their business will make money. If not, they move on to the next idea or project that will generate money. Your belief system will be tested throughout this process. Stay committed.

Belief Is Passion and Action

Passion, a highly charged emotion, can fuel you to work through the toughest periods. But passion is not enough; taking action is required. After all, if you are preparing for a test, you must crack open the book and study.

Passion is the emotion and the action is the result. My passion to write my first book was strong—but it was not strong enough to get me over the hump. I had to make it bigger than just me. The goal is to help someone else, but I needed to make the effort. At some point, I had to put in the time to make it happen. It was tough getting started, but I pushed through. Now, I am working on a series of books.

If you are new to entrepreneurship, making progress on your business ideas can seem overwhelming. The results can take a long time, or there may be steps that produce nothing. Over time, and with discipline, you can achieve results for your business. Belief is one of the strongest determinants of a successful entrepreneur.

Belief Is Giving It a Name

Entrepreneurs will give their business a name—an important step for legitimacy. This is a concrete step to getting started with your business idea immediately. Your business becomes real once you give it a name, a mission statement, a website, and business plan.

Entrepreneurs must first grasp the vision and then share it with the chosen audience. Start by taking notes—and give that business a name.

My first business name, Roberson Consults Group, was chosen quickly. The website for Roberson Consulting was taken, so Roberson Consults Group was the alternative. The other components of the business started with writing down a general plan, services, and basic start-up costs. To meet initial costs—a professional website and money to cover old debts—I took on a loan from my parents.

By working at the coffee shop and keeping costs minimal, I was able to give my business a clear identity. Later, I started giving some of my other ideas an identity to tackle in the not-so-distant future.

Belief Starts with What You Know

Entrepreneurs have skills to bring to the table—believe it. Even basic skills will count: typing, conversational skills, etc. Entrepreneurs learn what they are good at (and not so good at) by applying themselves in a number of disciplines.

Aspiring entrepreneurs may be able to look into familiar areas to start a business. For example, having years of experience in my industry helped me understand the regulatory needs of my clients— but it did not help me with running a business. As such, I had to piece together essential information and figure out if there was a business opportunity here. Once I saw the opportunity, I had to develop a business structure and other needed functions. This is not easy, but you must start somewhere.

Belief Is Visualization

Belief starts with a dream. The goal for all businesspeople is to build a well-oiled, profitable machine. You want a machine that operates the way you want it to—and perhaps even better.

My dream for a fully functioning business was to find an intersection of several interests: business, charity, travel, and investments. And I am doing this today.

Belief Is Accepting Responsibility

Entrepreneurs are owners with responsibility—they own the challenge. Starting a successful business will be one of the most challenging things that you can do with your life. It will be your responsibility to generate profit over a set period. With a job, the responsibility of making money is on the employer, not directly on you (unless it's a sales job for commission). No profit—no business. There is method to the madness of grasping the big picture.

John Ortberg, the pastor of the Menlo Park Presbyterian Church, wrote a book called *The Me I Want to Be*, whose last chapter is "The Glorious Challenge." The book is biblically based, but it can be used for general life-enhancing purposes. In short, I believe that we are meant to do something in our life—a challenge or mission as some would call it. This book is a great resource if you want to dig deeper into your calling and purpose.

Entrepreneurs are no different. The task is to connect our work with our purpose on this earth.

Belief Is Using Your Gifts

Entrepreneurship is a gift you are meant to use. Generating ideas and problem solving are some of my gifts that I use to help other people: my target market. You may be the type of person who was meant to be an entrepreneur. It doesn't serve any purpose to bottle up your ideas and never use them. Let them out. Whether the gift makes money is another thing—the market decides that.

Entrepreneurs must know what they need to get the job done. Understand what you want in business and go after it. Think about your gifts and how you can use them. There are many problems in this world, and perhaps you can help solve them.

Belief Is Gratitude

Entrepreneurs should appreciate their opportunities. The fact that you're able to read and demonstrate an interest in starting a business is a blessing. You're given an ability to grow by adding to your knowledge base.

Take an inventory of things to be thankful for today. Health is a blessing. Intellect is also a blessing. Personally, I believe in God's involvement in the whole process, what I refer to as the "10/90 Principle." It means you put in 10 percent of the work, and God matches it with the other 90 percent. The original 10 percent also came from God; he just lent it to you in the form of a gift to use.

Workbook Questions

What inspires you about starting a business? Tell your story.

_____

_____

_____

_____

_____

_____

What intimidates you about starting a business?

_____

_____

_____

What skills do you have right now to start a business?

_____

_____

What do you want to achieve with your business?

_____

_____

_____

What are your challenges to solve in business and in life?

_____

_____

_____

#2

Find Venture People

Entrepreneurship is about putting together the pieces of your business idea—and following up with venture people.

Entrepreneurship is an investment of time in securing skills, talent, money, resources, and connections. The first investor in any business is *you*. Entrepreneurs are responsible for finding their own market opportunities by talking with people. While building my first business, I found myself traveling to various places and making connections with all types of people. Finding the right type of people usually starts with a coffee meeting, phone/Skype conversations, and then a follow-up of some sort if there is a connection. Not all meetings are fruitful, but they serve a purpose: piecing together information, asking questions, and building a network that can come in handy later.

Meeting Venture People

Venture people are connected (directly or indirectly) into areas like tech, investments, manufacturing, real estate, and a number of other sectors. These people can be found in industries directly responsible for the high cost of living in certain regions, like Silicon Valley. This means that there is money in that area—a good area for business opportunities.

Even social causes or nonprofits need money to exist, which is why you see a flood of fund-raising activity in the Bay Area as opposed to some other parts of the country. High-ranking government officials (venture people) constantly do fund-raisers with other venture people in some of the richest areas in California: Beverly Hills, Woodside, Atherton, Marin County, and Orange County.

These are highly connected people who have built careers or businesses, and they can help you along your way. Reach out to them and ask them questions about the business-planning process. Before doing so, make a list of questions to ask.

Tip: Try to remember questions in your head as opposed to reading them from a list.

Industries with Venture People

Venture people include investment advisors, venture capitalists, technologists, media executives, tech professionals, government officials, educators, service providers in high-growth industries, attorneys, consultants, accountants, entrepreneurs, real estate professionals, actors, and artists. Venture people may even have direct access to money for your business. For instance, the Bay Area is flooded with investors, start-up capitalists, and venture capitalists. Find people who can help you get started.

Why Network?

Venture people are a resource for your business when you are looking for clients, customers, partners, affiliates, and money that you'll need for success. For example, if you are launching a start-up, it would probably make sense to connect with an attorney. If your business is in real estate, then hook up with an accountant. Also, you may need to reach out to other professionals using various channels. Try a meet-up group. This can be a great way to connect with other venture people. I go to events from time to time when it makes sense.

Networking is an art. Recently, I attended an Oakland event called "Classrooms2Careers," a youth job-placement initiative from the Oakland mayor's office. City and private industry professionals discussed the need for mentorship for Oakland's youth that are seeking employment. During the meeting, I took out my phone and used its notepad to take notes, something I always do to record topics of interest to me.

Time to Connect the Dots

Make a record of your conversations with venture people. The day after the Oakland meeting, when I went to a coffee shop to process notes and search for contacts on LinkedIn, I discovered a big mistake: I had forgotten to write down the names of the people who spoke at the event. "D'oh!" as Homer Simpson would say. Luckily, my business partner had taken notes and saved the day for me. A clear lesson: after having conversations with a venture person of interest, write down his or her name.

Tip: Write down information about venture people and figure out how each person fits into your ultimate plans.

Building a business is like putting together a puzzle. Get creative!

Think of an artist's portfolio of multiple paintings. *The artist is you.* That venture person may not be relevant today—but what about tomorrow? You never know when that real estate agent or accountant or even schoolteacher connection will come in handy. One business can consist of multiple customers, industries, or clients.

Follow Up with Venture People

Entrepreneurs *must* follow up with others for success. This is one of the most important things to do for your business. In fact, one of the most common compliments I received in my consulting business was about my level of responsiveness to my clients.

Entrepreneurs are bold. As a young person, perhaps in your transition years (eighteen to twenty-four or so), holding a conversation with a person of high intelligence or accomplishment can be intimidating. They may not come across as friendly, and you may not feel smart enough or think that you possess a certain level of sophistication to hold a business conversation. Get over it—this is your time to reach out and learn. If necessary, study a particular subject before reaching out to that smart and intimidating person. This is the time to show that you are smart.

Build Connections

Being an entrepreneur can be uncomfortable, but you can get stronger and gain more confidence by making connections with smart people. For you, the budding entrepreneur, it will take a willingness to go out and talk with people to build the network for your business. Connections made from my business reach all over the United States—and to a few places globally. Start small—around the corner if necessary. From there, you can start to replicate the process that successful entrepreneurs and many wealthy connections use.

The goal for many entrepreneurs is to build enough connections to make money and become wealthy. This may not be your goal, but having a wealth of connections is a worthy goal—you'll need it.

Wealthy People Seek Connections

Many successful entrepreneurs are wealthy venture people. They build portfolios of businesses and other income-producing entities such as real estate. Robert Kiyosaki, in his book *Rich Dad Poor Dad*, teaches us about these general principles. The investor (you) looks to build enough passive income, things that make money, like your business.

Venture People and the Coffee Shop

Venture people follow other venture people. Others may simply enjoy the taste of coffee or need that caffeine jolt in the morning, but many venture people have an objective in mind: work or hold a business conversation with people at the coffee shop.

Upon returning to the Bay Area and visiting places like Red Rock Coffee in Mountain View, I heard it all: conversations about start-up businesses, deals, investor pitches, and other business-related topics. These days, visit any metropolitan area and you'll find a lot of people handling their business at the coffee shop. I do because I am a venture person.

Workbook Questions

Who are some venture people you know?

_____

_____

What do you need from venture people?

_____

_____

_____

What can you learn about venture people?

_____

_____

_____

Where are the venture people?

_____

_____

_____

Why should you reach out to venture people?

_____

_____

_____

#3

Test the Business

A business will involve an equation(s) with several variables (issues) to solve…Plug in the variables and then make it (the business) better over time.

Like many students, I took algebra during the ninth grade. At the time, my teacher—we'll call her Ms. G.—would explain in her husky-from-smoking-cigarettes voice the methods for solving equations. As a self-conscious freshman, I found this period difficult. For me, these problems required extra work, including ongoing tutoring and extra time with Ms. G. There was a lesson here: preparation for the test. Similarly, for you as a student in business, your test is about gearing up to meet the requirements for starting a business.

The requirements are determined by the type of business you start. Ask questions. There are terms and procedures, such as crafting a business plan, that are outside of the scope of this book. This chapter is designed to get you to ask questions and write down a general blueprint of your business idea.

Entrepreneurs can build a business in many ways. For my first business, I researched other business models, tested out my services, and then created my first platform with this mission statement: serving the investment community to make a social impact.

My mission turned out to be a broad but specific enough statement to cross into all types of areas for my businesses.

Tip: A business model is designed for the successful operation of an idea.

Mission, Vision, and Problem Statements

A mission statement is a summary of the goals and values of a company, organization, or individual. A vision statement identifies what an organization wants to achieve over a period of time. A problem statement is a description of the issues that need to be addressed by the team.

Test the Value and Pitch

Entrepreneurs are limited in their ability to create value for their consumers, customers, or clients. Take an inventory of the possibilities that exist in today's marketplace for creating value. This chapter is about asking as many questions as possible to assess a value for your business. For example, your initial business idea may turn into multiple businesses. Before reaching this point, an important part of the planning process is to break down the components of the business.

Making a pitch is another method to test your business idea.

Tip: A pitch is presenting an idea before an audience.

Pitches can be used to gain a needed critique or to seek business opportunities. I've conducted a few practice pitches as a toastmaster, at a professional speaking organization, and at a few start-up events. Pitches can include items such as the problem, mission, vision statements, balance/income, marketing, and whatever data give your business an advantage, which is also known as the "wow factor."

Types of Business

First, understand what type of business you're going to start. Below are two examples.

1) **Product(s)-based business:** Consists of any physical item that

you sell to a customer or client in exchange for money. You make a profit when you sell it for more than you paid to purchase, produce, or deliver it.

2) **Service(s)-based business:** Consists of any service or method of giving something to a customer or client in exchange for money. As above, you make a profit when the price charged is above the cost of providing the service.

The Requirements

Attend a high school or college class on any given day, and you will be exposed to a great amount of material from an instructor. The instructor gives you an outline of what is required, and you take the necessary steps to deliver in the form of a book report, test, and/or homework.

The goal here is to gather resources to best prepare for the assignments. The equations you've certainly studied in school provide you with a some background to solve future business problems. Future business owners will face many challenges. Testing your business requires a certain amount of research, so start with a plan.

The Business Plan

Entrepreneurs make plans; this is a part of the testing process. For many, the way to express their ideas is through a business plan. Many people get bogged down in the process of filling out a fifty-or-so-page document. I view the business plan as an active document. While starting out of the coffee shop, I wrote down some of my plan, conducted research, and then went to market. I found that I didn't have everything figured out. After doing more research, I updated the business plan. For me, the plan is always active; it's never quite finished. If this sounds like your methodology, I would suggest writing down some ideas and then conducting a test for your market.

How? Ask a bunch of questions.

Entrepreneurs have to figure out what methods will work best in their planning process. For me, I figured out a lot by directly contacting my target market and then writing out the plan. You must figure out what works for you—and what doesn't.

Find Trends

Identifying hot trends or large-scale needs is gold to a business idea. A regulatory (government), environmental, technological, or some other type of rule change creates opportunities. The rise of social media and Google led to people needing help with Search-Engine Optimization (SEO) and social media strategies. Finding trends in your industry will help you gauge the needs of your target market. Many businesses have arisen from making products or services to address these core areas.

In my first business, I learned to spot trends by having direct conversations with my intended market (customers). Usually, I asked them a series of questions to gauge the market. My response was based on their answers.

Some resources can include surveys, think tanks, databases, and even social media. Facebook's ads manager has a huge database you can use to tailor your products for a particular audience.

Business Questions

Think about how you felt when you first learned about equations in algebra class. Like an equation, a business will involve several variables to solve. Questions to answer for the business will include factors, such as time, relationships, money, and start-up costs. These are issues that must be addressed for the business to succeed.

The following is a general guide to questions that you will need to address in planning your business.

Market Research

- What do people like?
- What do people need?
- Where do people visit?
- What do people eat or drink?
- Where do people go during the day?
- What do people do for fun?
- What are people likely to buy?

Products/Services

- What are your products?
- What are your services?

Time

- How much time must you spend on the business?
- What are ways to maximize/reduce your time?

Money

- How much money (capital) do you have?
- What amount of profit do you want to make?
- Will your profit be enough money to cover the basics?

Costs

- How much is this going to cost?
- Will gas prices affect your profit?
- What are your delivery fees?
- Are there any trademark or licensing fees?
- Any office and equipment fees?
- Are there insurance fees?

Liabilities (other costs outside of the business)

- What are your rent or mortgage costs?
- What is your student debt load?
- Any car payment or maintenance costs?
- Any personal insurance costs?

Location

- Where should your business operate? Do you prefer to be in your home state or another state or country?

The type of business you operate determines the location. My first business was located in the Bay Area, but it wasn't limited to only one region. With the help of the Internet and planning, my business was able to operate in other cities and states. Many businesses can operate in many cities as long as it remains possible to deliver a product or service. For instance, a service or health-related business may require an owner or a worker to visit customers. So for those with limited capacity, it may make sense to keep your business local.

Testing a business requires adding products or services that are favorable to that particular area. For me, a region with a concentration of wealth is usually a good place to start. Targeting a particular customer is another means of settling on a location. For example, a McDonald's that sells a McRib in Memphis may fare better than one that sells a McRib in California. People in one region may have different tastes than those in another region.

My Case History

Starting my first consulting business involved finding answers to questions directed toward my target market: investment advisors. First, while answering questions, I needed to figure out solutions to sell to clients in order to meet my income needs. Second, I needed to craft actual services and package offerings with prices (according to the market). Finally, I needed to figure out a way to deliver these services in order to get paid.

Once the first sets of questions were answered, the first website went up. Next came a three-month waiting game for my first client. Getting customers is an important step to validate the business since you need to make money to be a successful business. From that point, I had a legitimate business. After a four-year period, my first business grew to more than one hundred and twenty-five clients. Now there are two active businesses, a pending charity, four websites, and a book series in the works. Now comes the challenge of managing the growth in activity—a new set of questions to solve emerges.

Growing Pains and Expansion

It's 1:30 p.m., and the phone rings. I'm busy on a project, and no one else is around to answer my calls. I stop to answer it. This brings my current project status to a grinding halt. On any given day, I can be juggling phone calls, completing projects, researching, and handling the administrative components of running a business. For the solo shop, this can pose some problems—juggling too many functions. Although this was the case that day, I am thankful that my business activities are growing. With that said, constantly juggling the phone and project needs is not sustainable. As such, I must find ways to manage this growth with solutions—possibly a telephone answering service or an assistant.

Entrepreneurs may look at different ways to improve their business processes to avoid having to do everything. One way, *scale*, is about expanding your business so that components of it can run without your involvement (think of a franchise like Subway or a service like Facebook). At the right time, this can be an asset to the future value of the business. Technology solutions are most valuable when they can offer a degree of scale—think of one platform that can handle ten processes at once. As humans, we cannot do this, so we rely on some forms of scale to do this for us. Some business models can replicate their production process using scale, which is the ability to replicate a business process with some level of automation.

One problem is that consulting limits my ability to scale (expand my business without putting in more man-hours). In order to tackle this challenge, I have to look at technology solutions, hire outside consultants, or even completely outsource certain functions. I will talk a bit more about the growth process in the chapter on "Sales and Relationships" and go into more details in my later books.

Workbook Questions

What type of business do you want?

_____

_____

_____

What are some questions to start your business planning?

_____

_____

What are your initial concerns?

_____

_____

_____

What problems do you need to solve?

_____

_____

_____

What must you do to improve your business?

_____

_____

_____

What are solutions for your customers?

_____

_____

How will you execute on your plans?

#4

Focus on Results

Bootstrapping is not about having everything figured out; it's about the willingness to figure out everything that you need along the way.

What does it take to start a business? Tyler Perry, one of the most successful African American cinema entrepreneurs, posted a video on YouTube on "How to Be Successful." He said simply, "Start with one thing first." Since Perry is a successful businessman, his thoughts carry a good amount of weight. He grinded to get where he is today by starting with one thing: stage plays. From there he's built a media empire spanning numerous ventures. At some point, for success, you must move out of the planning process by setting clear objectives.

Goals and Benchmarks

Many successful entrepreneurs start with one thing first—and some stay with that one thing. There isn't one formula for success. One thing is for sure: hard work and an ability to sell your goods will be required. If you can't sell one T-shirt, then why should you add a clothing line? If you can't sell a line of clothing, then what makes you think that you should open a chain of retail stores? Set benchmarks for your business.

Setting and achieving benchmarks will help to build your work ethic. For your business to work, *the vision that you have must intersect with your work ethic.* Vision may be described as those moments when ideas pop into your head. Work ethic is a series of moves, sacrifices, and planning measures to get the job done.

Entrepreneurs have a vision of the finish line. As witnessed in the final scene of Disney's movie *McFarland, USA*, building a work ethic to run a race will require discovering your own pace. Runners will discover their pacing by taking time to practice. Run too fast and you get tired; run too slowly and other people lap you.

Don't Talk about It—Be about It

Entrepreneurs are always busy in the race to make a profit. In fact, the idea is to become so busy working on your ideas that by the time you look up, progress has been made. Focus on results so that you have something to show for the planning process. This is my mantra (goal) for working on various projects. In other words, I won't start talking about it unless I'm doing it. Otherwise, you can become a head case in failed actions. Some ideas get trashed, but over time I've built a track record for getting results.

Focus on Making Money

At one time, a popular song on the radio had the following line: "Stop wasting my time if it ain't about the money." Normally, I don't put much stock in popular songs, but this one has a point: entrepreneurs need to make money to be a business.

Similarly, remember the days, hours, and nights that you spent searching for your first job? Some of you may be in that process right now. It's not really what everyone told you it would be. Even so, you must press on to get that first check for the rent, a car payment, or the other bills that need to be paid. This is not a charge to become greedy (you should be the opposite—giving), but entrepreneurs understand that capital is required to operate, even when your aim is to help others.

Focus to Get Ahead—Not Behind

Entrepreneurs must step it up to become a producer, to receive more than they spend. An entrepreneur is in a race to get ahead of the bills. As a consumer, you will have bills. In addition, there are many other businesses attempting to sell you things every day. If you go to a hot dance club and get the urge to buy an overpriced drink—you got sold. You see a long line in front of an ice cream stand and want to buy ice cream—you got sold. See an ad for the latest shoes and you spend $120—you just got sold.

How do the producers win? They have ownership in something that generates money (more than they're paying out). They adopt a producer lifestyle: create, sell, or produce something to sell to other people. As a producer, you jump to the receiving end of consumerism.

We are all consumers—even those of us who live a minimalist lifestyle use resources. Wear clothes? You shop at a store. Need to get to work? You drive a car or take a bus or a train to work. When I need to purchase services for my business, I am a consumer for someone else's business.

Resist Distractions

One any given day in social media land, my inbox is flooded with comments, posts, and videos of people doing things. Dramatic news stories, YouTube videos, Facebook, and other forms of media can be important at certain times. Sometimes, even random phone calls will throw me off.

Entrepreneurs must focus harder to work because distractions can come from anywhere. An instant message appears on your phone or via social media. You keep checking your devices throughout the day, and then, all of the sudden, the priority work does not get done. Other distractions can come from friends, family, or others who fight for your time. They require attention, so you may have to make sacrifices. Sometimes it helps me to sneak away to a quiet place to get work done. If you don't focus, then the work won't get done, and *you won't get paid.*

Focus on Putting Projects in Categories

Small businesses have multiple responsibilities on a daily basis—from ordering supplies and making products to servicing customers. Put your work in categories; break down the projects. This helps me to make great progress. I will work on one project and then make time for the others based on my priorities.

Entrepreneurs plan different products to launch or start in different seasons. The book, T-shirt line, or app may take time to develop or perfect before it's released to the public. On any given day, I am taking notes (Post-it Notes are great) for a variety of projects. Some are short-term and others are not. There will always be periods to add, change, or modify your business in some way.

Avoid the nothing-to-do syndrome; there is always something to do to improve your business. If the idea is big enough, then there are always improvements to make. Sometimes when things are going well, it's easy to sit and coast on past successes. It's fine to take breaks, but don't get too comfortable. Work for more as there are always twists or unexpected turns in business. If you don't know what to do, it will be your job to get advice on steps you need to take your business to the next level.

Focus on Doing Well

One of my old roommates and friend, Tommy, is in charge of a campus ministry for college students. As a part of his duties, he is required to raise money for a living to support the work and his family. Raising support requires, among other things, advertising his efforts, sending e-mails, making calls, and reaching out to prospects.

In short, he is a salesman and entrepreneur but not in the traditional sense. His goal, or business objective, is to help college students by spreading the Christian gospel and meeting other immediate needs— a social entrepreneur of sorts.

Since college, Tommy has been able to raise enough support to continue doing good work for college students. Lesson: Sell to those people who see value in the work that you are doing.

Focus on Building Discipline

Working as an entrepreneur requires learning *how to work*. For most of us, our first working experiences in life were in school and in chores assigned by our parents. I remember that it was hard for me to see the benefit of school, a seemingly never-ending schedule that included the dreaded word *homework*.

The term *bootstrapping*, often associated with start-ups, means learning *how to work like a mad dog to get work done*.

In my more mad-dog days, while driving to a location, I would take calls in my car or try to push out competing assignments. Those of you who deal with multiple tasks, assignments, or jobs will understand the nature of juggling. It is hard, and sometimes it throws you out of balance—but that's life.

Bootstrapping isn't pretty; it's a "hustle" that will require more sacrifice than many are willing to give. Bootstrapping is not about having everything figured out; it's about the willingness to figure out everything that you need along the way.

Workbook Questions

What is one thing that you need to focus on?

_____

_____

_____

What are some goals/benchmarks you can make?

_____

_____

_____

What projects do you have to start?

_____

_____

What do you need to do to finish a project?

_____

_____

_____

#5

Sales and Relationships

Entrepreneurs must position their business for the sell.

Entrepreneurs understand that sales and relationships with their target audience are the heart of any business.

My first client found me on LinkedIn. What sold him were our commonalities: our similar work experience, my association with an investment firm he was familiar with, our travel stories (he was an airline pilot), our nonprofit work, and our city of residence (Redwood City). In fact, our first conversation was more about everything else than about his business needs. He needed to get a feel for me. This experience taught me that establishing relationships is a key component in the sales process.

Tip: Create a LinkedIn profile today.

Learn to Sell

Entrepreneurs must position their businesses for the sell. They can do this by making a platform that consists of 1) the product or service, 2) client relationships, and 3) the delivery system. A sale takes a certain number of steps. At first, I had to wing it on the sales process.

Tip: Selling will always be a hot skill. A master of the sales game will come up with a strategy to generate multiple streams of income.

Entrepreneurs will create a strategy. It may not happen during the business-planning stage but sometime after the implementation of a business idea. My first business started off with one sales approach and grew from there with practice and experience.

To summarize, entrepreneurs must look at every single angle to find sales for their business. They must create a strategy for everything, such as sales technique, marketing, accounting, targeting customers, delivery, partners, and much more.

What Are People Willing to Pay?

Entrepreneurs must make connections between their businesses and the market. For sales to happen, businesses must find out what the market (customers and clients) is willing to pay for their product or service—period. If a business's price is too high, the customer may go to someone who offers a better price. My market consists of people with the money to pay for my services.

Tip: It doesn't make sense to search for customers with no money to pay for your services.

The market wants value—most of the time. Don't expect everyone to buy from you just because you are young and have a baby face. That will work when you are selling lemonade but not as much as you get older. Also, don't expect someone to buy from you if you have a "good heart" and a "warm message." You must bring value to the table.

Marketing Value to Customers

A product or service must be valuable to customers—not just to you. The market wants to consume what it thinks will benefit itself in some way.

Tip: Consumers are those who use resources.

If you fail to convey value to consumers, they won't pay for your services. Find the value in your product or service to position your business for sales.

Entrepreneurs understand that proper marketing is essential. When no one knows that you exist, you don't get sales. What types of channels will you use to get the word out? Advertisements, social media, and a great location will help in this process.

The Delivery of Products or Services

Let's say your marketing is complete and the business has established a presence with its target customers. Next comes the delivery of goods or a service—making the sale. A customer orders a pizza and gives the deliveryman money when the food arrives. With good customer service and a tasty pizza, customers are likely to order it again for repeat business.

Let's look at the delivery process of a typical pizza joint: Domino's. A typical Domino's store is owned by a franchise. In most cases, delivery drivers use their own cars to bring the pizza from the store it's made in to the customer.

Tip: A franchise is an independently owned business under an existing corporate brand.

As owners have multiple priorities—even with a small business—they will need to hire a staff to deliver the pizza.

How the Business Delivers—Simplified

The delivery process (in no particular order) includes:
1) The manufacturers/suppliers make ingredients for the pizza.
2) The distributors bring ingredients for pizza to the business.
3) The business owner decides what list of products (pizza) to deliver.
4) The staff/business owner delivers the pizza.
5) The customer receives pizza and pays the delivery driver.
6) The business owner sells his or her products to resellers—other businesses that sell your products, such as supermarkets that sell Domino's frozen pizza.

Determine what is and is not relevant for your business-delivery system. For my consulting business, a service-based model, some of these things here are not relevant, such as manufacturer/supplier. In contrast, this book, a product under my other business, will have a manufacturer. There is not one set of processes; you must figure out the components for your own business.

Cross-Selling and Partnerships

Entrepreneurs use other businesses to sell products (and vice versa). This is cross-selling. For me, I use a book platform like Amazon to sell my product. In return, Amazon gets a hefty chunk of profit and access to customers who may decide to buy other products on the site.

Like Amazon, a business can act as the buyer (customer) and seller. The common terms for this relationship are *affiliate*, *reseller*, and *partner*. Similarly, the typical Starbucks may have products from other businesses. Starbucks resells the products in exchange for profits. As is the case for many large businesses, if the product is profitable, the large business may just buy out the producer of that product.

Entrepreneurs also can leverage one industry with another.

Tip: Leverage is like extending your reach to more audiences.

Another way to boost your chances of success is by linking with other industries. Maybe you can sell their products, or they can sell yours for a portion of profits. Who said you have to stick with one type of product for one type of market? Think bigger. There are many opportunities for forming partnerships, affiliates, or relationships with others when you're building your business.

Hiring Other Businesses

A great part of running a small business is that you get to help other businesses. When engaging new consultants, I look for their level of responsiveness first and then the work that they do next. Over the last four years, I have been able to hire multiple service providers to help me with my business ventures—at least seven and counting. It's a good feeling.

Understand Your Customer

Getting sales requires understanding the needs of the target customer. A relationship is paramount; your customers are human, not robots made up of artificial parts. You can build relationships by gauging the interests of your customers (through surveys, coupons, commercials, etc.) depending on the type of business you start. Getting the sale is great, but getting them to come back is even better.

Many product-based businesses won't establish close relationships with their customers. Selling a valuable app, code, patent, product, or scalable business model is a great way to make a lot of money, but in this model, focus groups or surveys may be most appropriate to build the business.

Service-based businesses (e.g., consulting, health care, etc.) require more of a relationship with customers. Customers don't always want to talk to a coded voice-answering system; they want personal interaction. Before reading your book, people want to establish some type of connection. In my first business, I started by establishing a relationship with customers. Often they were having difficulty with a technology or application, which prompted the need for a personal touch to troubleshoot the problem.

Cheat List—Mastering Sales and Relationships

There are three ways to better understand the sales process:
   1) Find the Need—What do people need?
   2) Find the Solutions—How can your business meet the need?
   3) Find the Value—What will people pay money for?

#1: Find the Need

Needs exist everywhere—find them. Starting a business is about identifying the problems of a particular customer. For instance, humans have a need to provide a source of energy for their bodies, so they eat. As such, we have supermarkets, co-ops, and restaurants to meet that need. We live in a society where people like to wear clothes—nice ones, in most cases—so they go to clothing stores to purchase them.

#2: Find the Solution

Entrepreneurs must figure out how to provide a solution. In doing so, they must create a business to meet this need. If you have a website selling food, do you have a way to record and deliver orders? If you have a store, do you have a supply of things that people want to buy? These are your solutions to a need.

One day I was meeting with my pastor for coffee, discussing my business model and how the church could help in our efforts. We began to discuss the greater needs of youth—mainly, what type of skills or programming would help them make it in Silicon Valley, one of the most expensive places on earth to live. This discussion was like an analysis to figure out what type of product or service would benefit the community.

#3: Find the Value

Throw your value on a plate for your client or customer. Before starting a business, the first thing you should ask yourself is "What value is this business going to give to our customers or clients?"

Business owners must discover something their target market

values. If the market doesn't value it—*you don't get money.*

Workbook Questions

Who is in your target market?

_____

_____

_____

How can you get in front of people?

_____

_____

_____

What is the value of your product or service?

_____

_____

_____

What are some sales strategies you can use?

_____

_____

_____

How can your business support other businesses?

_____

_____

_____

#6

Fail Forward

Apple is so successful because it makes products that are in demand, and it fixes its mistakes.

Failing forward simply means moving forward despite making mistakes (or mishaps). With starting a business, this process is similar to a baby learning to walk. At first, the baby will constantly fail in its earliest attempts to walk. With more practice, the baby continues to stumble but gets a little better and eventually learns to walk. In business, there are no guarantees for success, but entrepreneurs can use failure as a means to figure out what works and what doesn't work.

According to a study by StatisticBrain.com, the reasons some business owners fail include emotional pricing, living beyond their income level, nonpayment of taxes, lack of planning, no knowledge of financing, no experience in record keeping—and the list goes on and on.

Starting a business is a risk—but it's a necessary one for success. Silicon Valley is one of the most expensive places in the United States because people come from around the world to take the risk to start up something. Some people in Silicon Valley are doing quite well in business—even when beginning from the most adverse conditions.

Learn from Mistakes and Improvements

"Started from the bottom, now we're here" is a verse from a popular rap song. It's a part of my story—hitting rock bottom due to financial mistakes, which turned into the kick-in-the-butt moment I needed to make improvements. To become successful, I had to step up my work ethic—pushing harder than ever to make a plan to get paid.

As mentioned, my first client came eventually—about three months after I started the business. I took a risk: I borrowed money from my parents to pay off some debts and to help start the businesses. It worked, and I paid back my parents every cent of the loan—something to be proud of.

Entrepreneurs will find mistakes or things to improve in the business. Sometimes those mistakes will cost you money and clients—but that's a part of the process. Mistakes can be a good thing if they help you to know what to improve. With careful practice, you can use mistakes to make an efficient product or service. Just don't give up. I've made mistakes, but these have strengthened my business, helping me make a better product.

Apple's Changes

Look at Apple, one of the most successful companies in the history of business. It goes through a million updates to fix bugs (mistakes) in its OS programming and other applications. That means Apple makes mistakes—lots of them. When this happens, the company receives feedback from consumers

Apple is so successful because it makes products that are in demand, and it fixes its mistakes. Mistakes and feedback are valuable because a business won't know what to fix otherwise. No business will have everything figured out. It will make numerous iterations (changes), including changing its product design, pricing, content, and messaging—the list goes on and on. Don't let fear of making mistakes stop you from working on your business idea.

Failure Is High

A Harvard Business School lecturer estimated that approximately three out of four tech-based start-ups will fail. In business, if people aren't interested in your product, you can't generate any revenue. If business owners don't save capital, adapt, or anticipate changes, they may go through a period of struggle.

Failure is everywhere. Look on TV, the news, or in your personal life and you can see evidence of failure. Failure can be dramatic, sensationalized, or interesting. Media can even feed on the "moral failures" of celebrities. All money is not good money.

An entrepreneur can grow discouraged by watching the failure of others. How many people have talked about an idea with you and are still doing it? Or how many of you are around other people who are failing in life? Be careful not to internalize those failures.

People fail—that's life. If this is you, start again or quit—it's up to you.

My First Book Failure

The results of my first book were twofold. On one hand, it was a testament to beating five years of procrastination. The book found new life and expanded from its original purpose as a collection of my travel experiences in Africa and Asia. My first mistake was in losing most of the journal notes from my camping trip/teaching experience in Africa. Because of laziness, I forgot to back up my journal notes on my computer.

Even despite those mishaps, I was able to put the pieces back together. The book turned into a travelogue, autobiography, and personal journal, but it had no clear objective. As I result, I attempted to cram too much information about my life into one place. At the time, I wasn't sure of any one particular audience, and so my target was directed at all markets: youth, adult professionals, retirees, entrepreneurs, teachers, and everyone else. In business, it's a bad idea to attempt to cover all markets at once. Focus on one niche first, and then you may be able to add other people later.

The book did serve a great purpose—a victory toward putting all of my experiences together in one place.

Build Business to Last (or Sell)

Entrepreneurs will spend a significant amount of time to make things right. *Get this process down and you may not have to get a job working for someone else ever again.* Build a business to last over time, which will make it more valuable. Perhaps you will be able to sell it at some point, or just keep it and live off its profits.

Workbook Questions

What did you fail at (or overcome)?

_____

_____

How can you improve your business (after failure)?

_____

_____

_____

What lessons did you learn?

_____

_____

_____

Any good come from those moments of failure?

_____

_____

_____

#7

Manage Emotions

Managing emotions is an important component of the business-planning process.

Steve Harvey, a successful media entrepreneur who seems to be dabbling in everything dealing with entertainment these days, released a YouTube video on how to be successful. He equated the journey of success with the experience of jumping off a cliff. (Disclaimer: this is a metaphor, not a real cliff.) The art of success is in taking a risk that can feel as if you're jumping off a cliff with a parachute. The cliff can be your finances, career, lifestyle, or some other dramatic change. The parachute won't immediately open, but once it does, you can soar.

Harvey says that successful people make the move before the parachute opens. As such, they will have some scars along the way, but once the parachute opens, they soar. If you don't jump, the parachute will never open—and you will never soar.

Successful entrepreneurs will face a slew of emotions on their journey, which should not be ignored in your business. If you start a business but fail to control your emotions during the ups and downs, then you lose, as this can lead to destructive habits.

Emotional Triggers

Emotions are triggered by moments that exceed our comfort zone—periods outside of what's normal. Think about how you'd feel about graduating from school one day and then suddenly opening a business the next day—perhaps a little excited or nervous. In our lives, emotions can be expressed in forms of joy and peace, or they can show themselves in fear, envy, self-doubt, or other negative thoughts. Sometimes emotions will change once we experience moments of unusual success or failure or even shifts in our work demands.

Entrepreneurs often live out-of-balance lives with a steadily increasing workload and time commitments for their projects. Writing this book is a time-consuming (but worth it) process that leaves me out of balance. In fact, while writing this book, I also created four new websites—out of balance *again*. And then I started planning another business—out of balance *again*. This is the nature of entrepreneurship: workload surges that may require spending time away from friends and family. This may not be practical given your own situation. One thing for sure is that as an entrepreneur, you will have to juggle life's other priorities, which is outside the scope of this book.

Sober Thinking

It's no secret: all humans have emotions. Spending too much time dwelling on the past, present, or uncertain future can confuse your decision-making process. If you are an entrepreneur, things will constantly change and stretch your level of comfort. To cope, entrepreneurs should use a number of resources. Some people turn to their faith (I do) and pray or meditate, seek advisors, or consult with friends and family to keep their balance. Constantly gauge your emotional triggers and find ways to bring yourself back in balance.

Call it a hunch, but I'd say that many talented musicians and artists struggle with keeping their balance. Many turn to drugs and alcohol to cope with sudden attention, paparazzi, wealth, and an inability to live a "normal" life.

Michael Jackson was an extremely talented musician. He was

also known to be addicted to pain medications. Unfortunately, many other creative people have fallen due to addictions to drugs—the list is too long to name.

In one interview, Jackson talked about nights that he would have trouble sleeping because he was flooded with ideas. As a creative person, I can be flooded with ideas. While far short of the musical genius of Michael Jackson, I have had days when sleep was tough because ideas were spinning in my head. Ideas are a gift, but many entrepreneurs are frightened about exceeding their comfort zones. One saying that I use to overpower these emotions is that "God's grace is sufficient for me to think and act beyond my own understanding" (Proverbs 3:5).

Successful entrepreneurs don't get bogged down in and talk about their emotions; they work through them. Stay hungry and humble.

Overpowering Emotions

Ever feel weird after working on your "abnormal" ideas? I do all the time. If you're a movie fan, you may feel as if you're living in some weird reality like in the movie *The Matrix*. In reality, it's our brains attempting to cope with a stretched comfort zone.

Entrepreneurship is about knowing what you want in life and business. This is a powerful element not to be taken lightly. If you knew that your ideas could drastically change your future, would you follow them? At first, maybe not. Writing my first book almost didn't happen. In the beginning, I couldn't handle it, and so I made every excuse not to write. This procrastination persisted for five years—until I started over as an entrepreneur.

Find Your Weaknesses

Everyone has weaknesses. Entrepreneurs need to be aware of what theirs are. What's mine? Truth is, I'm afraid of success. This is my emotional challenge. I'm comfortable with a certain amount of success, but new opportunities get to me (even while writing this book). For years I would stir up a series of doomsday scenarios in my head concerning pending disaster with success. I start to feel as though I don't deserve it, and the emotional me is expecting failure. Then I go through a mental/spiritual process to understand that it is going to be OK. Emotions can be lies and make issues bigger than they have to be.

Frustrating Days

It's Tuesday, 5:17 p.m., and I am on the way to the Oakland area to participate in a youth program. The day was long and frustrating—not unusual for any entrepreneur. After a longer-than-planned conversation with a client and a longer-than-planned wait to have my car repaired—my day was done. One problem: my project was left hanging. D'oh! On another day, a problem with a client's software leaves me on the line for longer than expected. On another day, there are hiccups with my new website design, causing more delays. On another day, I make some simple errors in e-mail messages because I am trying to juggle too many things. At these moments, anyone may feel like driving to some remote area and screaming from the mountaintops. Overly dramatic? Yes! But get over it; this kind of frustration is normal for an entrepreneur.

Reading Books to Gather Thoughts

In high school and some of college, I hated reading books. It was a chore worse than dishes. It took everything in me to concentrate. It's quite ironic as now I am an avid reader and writer (no, this is not a ghostwritten book). Entrepreneurship is a great tool to help you grow up and become serious about success.

Reading *Your Killer Emotions* by Ken Lindner was an eye-opener. He has a concept called Personal Emotional Triggers (PETS). These are scenarios driven by our good and bad emotions. When negative emotions or temptations come, Lindner says we should use some sort of logic system (I'll add in prayer as well) to lead us back to making good decisions, which are referred to as our "Personal Gold": ideals, morals, and beliefs based on our value systems.

The Rules Change

Entrepreneurs make the rules as they go along, according to their market. Instead of relying on someone else, such as a boss or superior, to create your tasks, you do this yourself. I know it feels odd. It's a shift from the world you may have known before. You don't have a job title that defines a series of tasks anymore—you have many tasks.

Entrepreneurs must learn to retrain their minds. If you are successful, nothing is normal anymore. You may not get along as well with your work friends as you used to. For me, living in the Bay Area is cool, as there are so many entrepreneurs here. If you feel odd with your old friends, find others who are more like you.

The Art of Second-Guessing

The Bible says, "A double minded man is unstable in all his ways" (James 1:8). This means that at some point, you have to buckle down and overpower your emotions. Own them!

Entrepreneurs have to make a million decisions—some big and many small. They cannot afford to get stuck on the small decisions. To avoid this, you must learn to make smaller decisions very quickly to avoid the dreaded trap of second-guessing.

Second-guessing is an emotional nightmare. It is even worse when decisions begin to bottle up from delayed responses or from making no decisions at all. Learn to make quick decisions, as this is crucial for success.

As an entrepreneur, you have only a small window to make

multiple decisions—the more success, the more decisions to be made.

Emotions When Working Alone

Starting without a business partner? You're not alone. According to the US Small Business Association's Office of Advocacy, 70 percent of small business are operated and owned by a single person. That means one person (you) is performing many tasks. Solo means you aren't going out with coworkers for lunch, attending holiday parties with coworkers, or spending days in meetings with coworkers. You are a one-person party. Get over it.

There are plenty of opportunities to be around other people. Visit a coffee shop or a coworking facility, which I often do. Today, I have a business partner to meet with, and that helps.

Emotional Outlets Are Necessary

In the beginning, most entrepreneurs work like mad dogs to get their business up and running. Naturally, this creates stress, which must be let out in different ways, such as exercise or just relaxing. Take time out to talk with friends and family, or do activities that are not related to your business.

Workbook Questions

What are your emotional triggers?

_____

_____

_____

What motivates you about your business idea?

_____

_____

What gives you anxiety about your business idea?

_____

_____

_____

What are some ways to deal with these emotions?

_____

_____

_____

#8

Find the Money

Finding money means finding people with money.

When they build profitable businesses, entrepreneurs are rewarded with money. Invest some time into helping your business grow, and it can become a source of long-term income.

Tip: As an owner with a profitable business, you may be able to sell it at some point—which means more money for you.

"What's the quickest path to money?" one of my advisors asked during a meeting about my charity goals. I didn't have an answer for him. In my mind, I was just going to create a charity fund and give away money—which is not a business plan. There was no path to the money. At some point, I decided to give the charity a try as a business. I didn't know how to get the money here—or even have enough traction to do so—until I found a partner to help with my efforts. Starting a legitimate business is about the race to get paid.

More Money Than Expenses

To start a business, even a nonprofit, you will have a number of upfront costs. Often you will spend a considerable amount of time and money just to start. At some point, the entrepreneur must be able to recoup the money spent. Remember, it took me months to find a paying client after establishing my first business. The faster you can deliver a product or service, the faster you can get paid.

Finding Money in Research and Data

Finding money means finding people with money. One way to do this is by conducting surveys to locate that target. One day while I was volunteering at an Oakland social enterprise, the young participants did that very thing—they sent out MailChimp mailers to students to find the market that is likely to cut a check. Either find it yourself, or pay someone else to get that data. Other ways to find your intended market are through the Internet, social media, trade associations, government sites, and other data sources.

Finding Money in Market Size

Finding money means finding a big market. In other words, the market you're targeting should be big enough for your business to make money.

Got coffee? According to the latest National Coffee Drinking Study from the National Coffee Association, 40 percent of those between eighteen and twenty-four years old drink coffee every day. Coffee drinkers outnumber tea drinkers in the United States: 183 million coffee drinkers to 173.5 million tea drinkers. These data tell me there is a huge market for people like me in the coffee business.

Five Ways to Make Money

Below are five different ways you can break down the money component so it makes sense for your own business.

Selling/Marketing

In marketing a product or service to a customer, the business's main objective is to get the other person to buy the item(s). Sales and relationships are the most important part of a business, so I dedicated a whole chapter to this subject. Types of marketing include print (newspaper), e-mail, online, in person, ads, commercials, and social media.

Trading

In middle school, my friends and I would trade basketball cards, baseball cards, and Blow Pops with each other. At the time, we were placing a value on these items, usually for money or for other items (trading). Trading is a game of strategy for a product-based business: buying a good (or service) at one price and selling it at another. The objective is to finds ways to convince someone to pay more for the product than you paid for it (profit). When you sell the product for less than you paid for it, you have a loss.

Healing

A doctor in a hospital attends to patients' health-related needs. A home health-care business sets up shop for the elderly. A pharmaceutical company hires a staff of scientists to research possible cures for cancer. Healing is valuable to humans. As such, there will be a need for these businesses as long as people get sick—and a need equals money.

Coding

The tech community—made up of coders, programmers, investors, financial professionals, and start-ups—works to find scalable solutions to business problems. Technology is valuable because it can attract large-scale buyers. The business can generate money from customers by selling data, selling its technology to others, or selling itself in a buyout. This happens often among Silicon Valley start-ups. Coding, matched with a business idea, can position people to create all types of scalable businesses. Even if the business fails, skilled coders can demand a high salary and easily find other job opportunities.

Scaling

Fred DeLuca, founder of the Subway chain, started a franchise to scale the Subway brand in locations around the world. Each franchise is operated either by a management team or a franchise owner, without requiring DeLuca's presence. The product is delivered, and he receives a portion of sales from all Subway stores—a business that expands to make more money.

When The Money Is Funny

Money doesn't grow on trees for any business. At the start-up phase, depending on the type of business, you must expect to weather a period of dry spells. The length of time to make a profit can be months or even years. This can be a tough time for those who don't have funds to weather the storm because those bills don't stop coming.

The best way to weather a financial storm is to work on other ideas when one idea isn't working. In addition, you may need to reduce your expenses and, if necessary, have supplemental income. There is nothing wrong with having other work while building your business—that is a badge of honor.

Keeping the Money

Entrepreneurs plan for the days when money comes in. When this happens, watch your books carefully. No one, outside of an accountant, bookkeeper, or spouse, will be there to watch the numbers for you. With success, you will begin to have people pitch their services to you. It doesn't matter how much good you do; if you don't watch your numbers, your business won't last. Capital is necessary for business growth—period.

Workbook Questions

Where's the money for your idea?

_____

_____

_____

What's the quickest path to money?

_____

_____

_____

What method can you use to make money?

_____

_____

_____

How can you keep the money coming in?

_____

_____

_____

How can you grow into other areas?

_____

_____

_____

#9

Get Advice

Listen to your customers if you want to stay in business. Great advice can come from customer feedback.

One of my first clients told me something that shifted my thinking in terms of business. He said, "I don't think in terms of hourly wages." Huh? I thought. Before thinking of offering services in the form of deliverables (services based on items completed), I put together a proposal for hourly contract work. Now I was asked to put together a package of services for him to consider. This advice was super-super-valuable to me. It got me to think more like a business owner instead of someone doing contractor work.

After that visit, I began to shift my business into a more efficient pricing method: a list of services in tiers similar to that of a McDonald's combo meal. I noticed that one of my largest competitors also had a combo-like pricing structure in some of its offerings. It made a lot of sense to me to move in this direction. In the end, changing my pricing structure made it easier for clients to choose—which meant more sales.

The person who gave me the advice not to price services by the hour was a venture person, a successful entrepreneur who makes investments in other businesses. I listen with both ears to people in high positions. Qualified advice is always great, especially from those who are successful because they know what it is like to run a business.

Finding Mentors

The most valuable business advice will come from those with no bias or clouded emotional attachment to you. They tell you what you need to hear. These people are mentors.

Mentors are people who can 1) hold you accountable, 2) give advice, 3) provide much-needed direction to your business, and 4) provide a clear example of what goals to work toward. Mentors can be formal (people you seek out) or those you observe, admire, and desire to emulate. Some of my mentors are people I've watched and learned from over the years. Try to find good people who are already around you.

Mentors can also be role models—that is, people you want to emulate in some fashion or seek out for advice. Chances are that you know someone who could serve in this capacity: an older professional in your community, a successful friend, or referrals from your LinkedIn network. Perhaps this is a person you watch get up every morning and provide for his family, or a friend with an inspiring story of perseverance, or a grandparent who helped raise you.

Customer Feedback

Great advice can come from customer feedback. A great piece of advice is to listen to your customers if you want to stay in business. I pay attention to my customers' comments, especially the few complaints I have received. Use surveys, Yelp, or another method to track the opinions of your customers. Be coachable. I listen to the advice of my clients. For my latest ventures, I have sought the help of three advisors and a few consultants along the way.

Advice from Reading Good Books

Read…please, read something. Reading is vital to starting a business. You find out what you need by reading and researching. In high school I hated reading, but now that it's essential for success, I love it. Reading is your chance to get ahead of the curve. When people told you that it's not cool to be smart or to read, they lied.

Why read books? Books are excellent sources of advice. For me to become a better writer or to present information to my clients, I had to read books and other publications. Other sources of advice can come from school, parents, counselors, or community-based leaders.

Dealing with Criticism

Some advice will feel like a knife in the gut. There may be days when criticism or negative comments from others will stir your emotions. Some criticism may be constructive and help you become successful, especially customer feedback. Other advice may be from "haters." These people may not understand or may be uncomfortable with your goals, and therefore they may make comments to diminish the progress you've made. Move past this; your assignment is to help your target customer.

Workbook Questions

What advice do you need?

_____

_____

Who do you need to receive advice from?

_____

_____

_____

What advice should you plug into your business idea?

_____

_____

_____

What type of material do you need to read for your business?

_____

_____

_____

Will you apply advice and suggestions?

_____

_____

#10

Have Fun

For entrepreneurs, success comes when they begin to love what they're doing.

Entrepreneurs understand the word *stress* all too well. As you probably grasped from reading this book, starting a business involves a million small steps; once you start you have to figure out what you need. Stress can build, and the amount of work can make you want to pull out your hair—but it's going to be all right. Be grateful that you have something to work toward: a lifestyle that you will enjoy.

For entrepreneurs, success comes when they begin to love what they're doing. They won't love everything, but if the big picture excites them, then they're on the right path. Perhaps it's your mission or the fact that you can make a living from your own ideas—enjoy it. If you can't enjoy any part of the business, you should seriously ask yourself if you want to stay in business.

Ultimately, the goal for entrepreneurs is to work and enjoy the fruits of their labor. Who wants to be stressed out all the time? At first, entrepreneurs have to go through the fire: stress, long nights, and sacrifice. Business owners have to develop a till-the-end-of-the-earth mentality, meaning they are willing to go the extra mile for success.

Entrepreneurs Become Heroes

Entrepreneurs, in my humble opinion, are the heroes of our

economy. They sacrifice time to create new opportunities for other people in the form of jobs, contract work, business relationships, and a host of other things. If my clients didn't have the guts to set up their businesses, I wouldn't have business. As such, if you've worked hard enough for results, then you get to enjoy them at some point.

Take time to have fun while building your business. Two ways to do this are to fit in activities that you enjoy and to go on a vacation if you can afford it. If you can't afford it, try to go to a place that helps you to relax, perhaps a nearby town. Be creative.

It's Fun to Create

My creative juices flow best while I am traveling from coffee shop to coffee shop. These are cheap places (with Wi-Fi) to work on my business, but something else has happened there as well. Coffee shops are where I became inspired to work on my charity-turned-business and on my first book. Visiting these places has become a tradition, an activity that keeps me motivated to work on new ideas. This is the space where ideas flow out of my head and onto paper. On other days, to balance stress, I'll go to random places to turn up the music and just dance and keep my spirit youthful.

Find your groove!

Workbook Questions

What do you love to do?

_____

_____

_____

_____

_____

_____

What do you love about your business idea?

_____

_____

_____

Book Series: *Don't Play Around, Write It Down*™

What do you do when you have more than one idea?

If you are really good at structuring one business, then you can build the skills to do the same with other businesses: serial entrepreneurship.

Stay tuned for the next book in my series.

Resources/Materials

Build Ur Impact has resources available to support and motivate you to start a business:

Website: www.buildurimpact.com
Blog: http://blog.buildurimpact.com
Questions? info@buildurimpact.com
Resources: www.buildurimpact.com/resources

Thank You

Special thanks to the first donors who supported our work before our enterprise was in its infancy:

Thank you for taking the time to read this book. We hope there are tools here you can use to market your business.

Thank you to Jesus Christ and to my family, friends, and associates for their support in writing this story.

My Transition

My transition started with a boatload of debt. While in Los Angeles, I was living in denial following a wave of poor planning, with losses from bad investments and insufficient income. Next came a period of living off credit card cash advances. Close to bankruptcy, I moved back to the Bay Area to start over—ready to give up on my dreams.

And so I headed to the coffee shop to work on a plan: apply for career jobs and find side work. At first the money came in small spurts from after-school programs. The problem was the money barely covered my gas bill. Frustrated, I decided to give entrepreneurship a try. The process started with notepads and without paying clients. No bueno!

What happened in the next three months was providence. I got my first client. Over a four-year period, my first business grew to more than one hundred clients. Now there are two active businesses, a pending social enterprise, a charity, four websites, and a book series in the works.

Do you have debt or some other challenge? You can make your way through it just as I did.

This is my story.

ABOUT THE AUTHOR

Cory Roberson is a businessman, investor, social entrepreneur, and author who spent over ten years working in the investment-management industry and with various social causes. In his first business, Roberson Consults Group, Cory has worked with more than 125 investment management firms across the country. As a social entrepreneur, Cory has volunteered with more than ten community service and educational programs serving youth around the world, including youth programs in California, China, and South Korea. In his second book, *From Student to Entrepreneur: Making a Transition to Business,* Cory shares **10 tips** for starting a business based on his own experiences.

Cory is founder of **Build-Ur-Impact,** a social enterprise geared toward supporting youth with entrepreneurship and life skills. He is also principal of **Roberson Ventures Group,** a portfolio of B2B affiliates. He is always looking for his next business ventures (coming soon). Cory is a graduate of the University of California, Davis.

Notes

Notes

Notes

www.ingramcontent.com/pod-product-compliance
Lightning Source LLC
Chambersburg PA
CBHW070843180526
45168CB00002B/935